BILL'S FORMAL COMPLAINT

BILL'S FORMAL COMPLAINT

DAN KAPLAN

The National Poetry Review Press
Aptos, California

The National Poetry Review Press
(an imprint of DHP)
Post Office Box 2080, Aptos, California 95001-2080

Printed in the United States of America
Published in 2008 by The National Poetry Review Press

978-0-9777182-5-2

Cover photograph by Ali Ender Birer

Author photograph by Susie Steele

CONTENTS

IV.

V.

for
Susie and Stella

Never trust biographies. Too many events in a man's life are invisible.

—Anne Michaels

I.

HELLO, MY NAME IS

Bill. Let me guess: you knew a guy named Bill
which makes it tough to picture other Bills.
The question is: who doesn't know a Bill?
Bill minced your heart in kindergarten. Bill,
litigious prick, missed the bottom step. Bill
the shih tzu–pomeranian mix. Bill
the vermiculturist. Mechanic Bill,
who murdered Santa. Did you know that Bills
are big in history? There's Pecos Bill,
Big Bill Broonzy, Bill Bixby, Pitchfork Bill.
Elizabethan England: lousy with Bills.
And earlier, the Conqueror. *William*,
you say. But can't a famous guy be Bill
outside the book, gnawing on a drumstick?

II.

TODAY #1

Today you are the man your mother pleaded
you not become: all but skin, all pleats
and Brylcreem, plunked borsalino, shocked teeth,
the world's joints sore at sight of your frailty,
embodiment of what you eat at Luby's,
healthy portion of yellow, unborn meat
warming over under that heavenly
heatlamp glazing the path to your bookie
who, steel-fingered, indulges your antique
idea of doing business honestly,
face to face, transactions only complete
with a handshake, leg-breaker with empathy
for you, who bets today on the ponies,
tomorrow a far cry from sleep.

BILL'S DREAM

Ordinarily I wouldn't mention it
but this has been a draining week.
I haven't once dreamed
anything of consequence.

But that can be draining too, week
after week of dreams that make
everything of consequence:
a chicken in orbit, an armless orchestra.

So after weeks of dreams of making it
with Kim Novak in *Vertigo*,
a chicken in orbit and an armless orchestra
tumble into dreams like sweaty strangers.

Because with Kim Novak in *Vertigo*
the dream is clean, sketched:
a tumble with a dreamy, sweaty stranger.
Pinch yourself. You're dreaming.

But sketchy dreams really clean you out.
Maybe all dreams are that way. Maybe Kim didn't deliver,
which puts you in a pinch:
was it simply you in Jimmy Stewart's well-pressed suit?

Dreams *are* that way. Kim didn't deliver
and surely you didn't pluck her from that steeple anyway.
It was simply you in Jimmy Stewart's suit, well pressed
to reckon why Kim donned a miner's helmet for the fire-
        place scene.

You don't have the pluck for Kim anyway. Sure, you
        stipulate
waking from dreams is like losing a rough argument
but reckoning why Kim donned a miner's helmet for the
        fireplace scene
and ate lettuce in bed

is the rough wake from the dream, the lost argument.
I'm sorry. What are we arguing about? A dream?
A bed of lettuce?
How did this one start again?

I'm sorry. A dream is like an argument
you couldn't dream up,
the one where you're arguing again
with someone who wouldn't ordinarily mention it.

THE DEFINITION, MORE OR LESS, OF BRAINWASH

lifted from *Dorland's Illustrated*
Medical Dictionary, 28th ed.
\breyn´wahsh´\ *vt* -ed/er/ing/able:
1. A systematic effort meant to plant
convictions on the west side of the hill
<Shall I ~ you? Dried or cut arrangement?>
2. Any cranial examination
(esp. custom hat [or at least headband] sizing)
or half-hearted poke at trash collection
3. To rinse the matter of preservatives
<Must I do everything around here?>
4. The simple act of thought delivery
5. The simple act of thought delivery

BILL TRANSLATES SWEDISH

Consider selling those begonias, petunia.

The train travels toward the border. Over there is a lake. The mountains are full of honey. Big and little children both ski.

Lars is here to speak with Lisa. Lars gets a ball from Lisa. That candy was fairly good. Lisa sleeps on the couch with her cats.

How much fun it is to have a lot of people around.

He eats his pear, she wears her bracelet, he has left his homeland. Come and look at these bears. Come along, even if you are tired. Even we are tired already. Let me get a look at you before you die.

A year goes by so fast. We are living here from now on. The decision came from the stairs.

Look, here is the newspaper. When dad comes home, we will eat him. May I borrow your blouse.

Those books are big. Do you want a transplant. If you are nice, you will get a transplant.

Would you be so kind as to go shopping for me. I have

fallen asleep.

The man is not nice. The woman is not old. He is not nice, though ugly. He goes outside with his dog. It is so nice in the sun.

Eva, who is a secretary, lives in Norrköping. Maybe we could study together.

Will you be my husband. Maybe you want to go home instead. I suppose you do not have any trees left.

How clever you are, big girl. I bike over you on the path. So sad that you are sick.

Could there be someone knocking on the door. We have dresses in our suitcase. Whatever you do, don't.

She puts them in her backpack and brings along her apple, too. She learned of it through me. She believes more in me than in you.

I must eat something. Have you eaten already. Unfortunately, we are not hungry right now.

Yes, I noticed that, too. Come, then we can eat.

He stands on the chair, there is salt on the table, there are clouds inside. We are living here from now on.

Tara,

Met a guy on the subway today
who braved to ask my name. No monkey
business so don't you worry. Nothing
squirrelly about him. The littlest things
I said made him laugh like a frank furnace.
And I love that. Don't know the last
time this transpired: swaying like a side
of beef and the good butcher takes a stab
at intimacy, a jewel of sweat
breaking on his clean, burned temple…

I know, I know. When you and I next talk
he'll be memory, a ruby planet snuffed.
But I tell you it's changing, my luck.
Oh, if you see Steve, tell him to fuck off.

C.

HAMMOCKED, BILL

I wave them on and still the clouds don't act,
just bare their hairline fractures like victims
of an authorless crime, an atmospheric
crash. Let's just leave it at that. These cosmic
types are everybody's star witnesses.
In this stratosphere, Pluto may be little
more than a chalk outline, but the battered
cumulonimbus is this close to giving
up Tropical Storm Edgar, which never
even touched it. And that's vindication
under the bright lights, that's evidence.
Some will spill guts for a cup of java
or gust of wind in the interrogation
room. Anything at all to build a case.

BILL'S FORMAL COMPLAINT

If mother hadn't fed me with that busted
spoon, I'd be hilarious now. And given
proper chance, I could cleanly shuck
the sharkskin pants off a runway model,

be more than *Man with Sunburned Ankles*,
clouds pressed against his back, the lone
man with sunburned ankles hacking through back-
yard tangle to excavate his spine. Damn dog.

I skipped another day of work. I await
the haggard landscape to shake itself off,
become something's anatomy. I loot
the trash for last night's chicken bones

and when I find them, I think it is the hips
I'm splitting. So I stop wishing.

JOAQUIN WAS DOWNSTAIRS IN THE KITCHEN AGAIN

with the long thin matches, burning my dreams. Charred essence of ghostly oceans, orbiting bricks, Buicks in trees wafted through the vents. Shit, I said and threw off the covers. By the time I reached him he was feeding the orchestra to a blue flame. I tripped on a cymbal, drove him off with the hose, then, composed, turned it on myself. In the Yellow Pages under pest control only mothers, hovercrafts, karma, and fjords were bulleted. And I had nothing against Norway. And all was settled.

SONG

At one time or another you'll behold
the fibers singly, feel the pasture
swallow, the windows screaming, you'll locate
midnight nosing through the dark in search
of food. You know the possibilities.
The other morning you were late, you pulled
a couple concentrated breaths and sealed
your eyes, your mind—a taxi surfaced
at the vanishing point. This is less
cause/effect, more so what you read.
Take this city. Long and brick and frosted.
On certain streets when the Olds breaks fifty
a music starts, the syncopated drum
of tires on grooves, the lead-in.

1. **A prospective employer asks why you left your last job. The truth: you got the boot. You say:**

    a. "I don't work for anyone who doesn't value truth."
    b. "I got fired," hoping your probity scores points and nobody asks what probity means.
    c. "Ever been to Cancun?"

2. **Is it important to you that people find you mysterious?**

    a. Yes.
    b. No.
    c. Perhaps.

3. **How much of "you" do you bring into your work space?**

    a. On your desk you have two photos of yourself at roadside, a brushy emptiness behind you. In one, you confront the lens; in the other, you shirk it; in both, you're equally foreign.

b. None.

c. Tons.

4. **You get tipsy at a party and tell a stranger your life story. The next day, you:**

   a. find him/her before he/she smears you/you.

   b. forget you ever spilled your guts.

   c. come up with a new one for the next stranger.

5. **How often do you swear other people to secrecy after sharing something private?**

   a. Always. Better safe than sorry. The question though: what's private? Your journal entries about foxglove? What about hand jobs? Are they private?

   b. Rarely, because you trust everyone.

   c. Never, because people usually stop listening before you finish.

6. **Do you ever lie to people so they find you more interesting?**

   a. No.

b. Sometimes.

c. No.

7. **When you talk about yourself with people, do you watch their faces to gauge how much to dish?**

    a. No, because people never want specifics.
    b. No, because people always want specifics.
    c. Yes, because people always want specifics.

8. **How do you feel about the moon?**

    a. The what?
    b. It's alright.
    c. I don't want it on a Triscuit or anything, if that's what you mean.

9. **Ever killed anyone?**
    a. Yes.
    b. No.
    c. Ever been to Cancun?

10. **When you're indecisive, is it easy to read?**
    a. Yes.

b. No.

c. I don't know.

III.

BILL

In a frayed wool sweater Bill with a sword splitting
a coconut FedExed from Hawaii. Bill perched on
a barstool, joints throbbing, rain pounding the tin
roof. *The Wizard of Oz* on Bill's black-and-white set.
Bill thrown to the pavement. The sun, as though
shot into the sky from Bill's finger. A woman
whispering "Bill" to herself, divvying the dog-eared
paperbacks. Bill asking the couple to sit down, their
faces uncommitted. The highway unspooling, Bill
reclining. Someone screaming "Cedric!" from across
the street in a new town. Red-eared, pelted by hail,
Bill studying the numbers on the house. Bill's hairless
cat, sunburned, found in the gutter by another kid.
The book of baby names left open at the V's.
Bill tipping a thick-thighed female impersonator
with an outstretched garter. A gaunt physician, two
years from retiring, handing Bill a prescription. Bill
giving a last over-the-shoulder look. Two-o'clock
appointment with Bill scratched out on the calendar.
"Bill" stitched in cursive red letters on the breast
pocket of a shirt worn by a teenager who never
knew Bill. A woman Bill hardly knows opening the
front door. The two-person bathtub in which Bill
once had three people. Bill on a first visit to the
ward, scanning the list on the wall. Bill's picture of
a tearful Pope in drag accepting the Miss Universe
crown. Bill, cold. The moon like a butter pat in the
southern sky. A line winding around the corner, Bill
near the end. Bill seeing an ad for something called
"yoga." Someone screaming "Bill!" in the terminal,
everyone looking.

ORDINARILY #2

Ordinarily I wouldn't mention it
but this has been a draining week. Not once
I've dreamed about the rollerskating shirt-
less violinist felling phone poles with

his bow who nonetheless performs flight
of the bumblebee. Why is this soothing.
The bees do not make honey, which I like,
and no one on the block can order in

Chinese, which many people eat and speak
throughout China, where I'd like to dream
or dream about. The dream never varies,
only the piece. Who said that? Or maybe

it goes recurrence is comfort and curse.
That's it. Recurrence is comfort and curse.

TODAY #2

Today you drape yourself across the fire
escape. You are an ageless, thin but iron
immigrant. You have the muscle shirt,
the solitary chest hairs, glistening forearms,
hand-rolled cigarette and you salvage stray
tobacco strings from tongue and teeth.
If the sky at evening is a washcloth
dripping color up and down a skin-

tight city chock with others snug in grids
of sweaty windows, you don't see it. There is
you, ashing. Shaking loose of record and scent
you stepped off a skiff to meet a fate in
trench coat. You knew you'd only ever own
the things you tucked beneath your skin.

PLATE 1: AN ANATOMY

A, plush spotless aqua den carpet; *B*,
you lying on it; *C*, your bones coasting;
D, stratocumulus cloud hung between
6th and 7th rungs of snowy rib;
E, chrysanthemum sprung from liver bed;
F, electroencephalographic
winch controlling larynx; *G*, hamster
wheel; *H*, hamster; *I*, rusted mufflers
ditched in the ear canal; *J*, spiders
in their spinal climb; *K*, capillaries
in the lap lane; *L*, boxes of soaked
tissue clogging up the storage unit.

See also *Essential Hemorrhage* (Plate 5)
and *Structural Deformation* (Plate 9).

BILL TRANSLATES HUNGARIAN

I am hungry. Would you like me to eat.

Opposite the vista is midnight. Midnight is dripping with something bright. Within 2 days it will be midnight again.

We accidentally lost the sea. It was here yesterday. It was damaged when we arrived. Someone will be needed to clean up.

Could you repeat that please. Where do I put the rubbish.

The stopcock is dripping. How do I shut off the stopcock. The stopcock will not stop dripping.

Where can I feed a baby. Do you have one in a larger size.

I need a shower in the morning. May I have an artificial sweetener in it. Otherwise, one cannot taste the skin.

Shall we get some fresh air where the water crashes. There are so many pieces.

I cannot eat these. May I have the shank. How

much longer will it be. I'd like paté in aspic, but bring me a beetroot now. Is cervix included.

You're fantastic. I'm with a group. I have only the normal allowances.

Please do not track glum inside. Everything is so clean. What bright colors in the eyes. Could you repeat that please.

What is this currency called.

Lay off. They will crack if you clank them like that.

I would like to declare that you need help in the field. This is one of the common opinions.

Is this the right platform for departing.

How many times a day. The buses disappear in the heat. The people switch feelings in the terminal. There are so many lives. How long will I have to wait for a connection.

I am of the opinion that you are getting smaller. I think your parents should check their baggage.

Where is your birth. You seem to have forgotten which compartment has been reserved for you. Go that way and then keep going and look. You may always ask someone.

Could you alter this. I would like it to fall all the way to the floor. I have many of them.

You are allergic to them. Have you ever been stung by one. I have and fell out of the rowboat once. Have you ever been swimming.

Yes, I have been swimming. Can you feel water beneath your skin.

Does it hurt when I do this. Does it hurt when I do this. How about this.

Is there someone else. Are there other people. May I visit you. I want to attend a happening.

BEEEP

Hello. This message is for Bill, the last
I'll leave. I know that you don't know me
but hear me out, please. I appreciate
the throb of being axed—there really
is no backswing, is there. Trust me, I've donned
that wig before. I've had to start again,
suture neck and throat and thaw the frost.
It sucks. But you should do the same, my friend.

I guess those are the last of my supply
of pearls. Question: couldn't you prophesy
this end? The steps were deafening. I pulled
your files. What exactly did you do all day?
So what I'm trying to say is this: will you
please get your shit out of my cubicle?

MIDNIGHT KITCHEN

The row of apples takes a hairpin turn
to pulpy, a Marciano pulpy,
but I refuse to credit even a germ
of life's truths to produce, especially

the biblical kind. This is not to say
there are not days I locate genuine
truths within my kitchen: the walls a frail
divide between mine and other lives

is one, the joy of bright frosting straight
from the tube another. Refrigerator
hum unbuckles yet another midnight.
The space between me and the lover

I don't have has grown. Her L-shaped room
is heated well. She's curled up like the moon.

THE LOVE LIFE OF BILL

13.

Bill had never been in this position before but could tell she had. He thought about baseball.

1.

Bill had gotten too heavily into his father's Brylcreem but smelled good. His slacks rubbed against his thighs as he paced his room waiting for 7:15. Through the floor he heard his father complaining about being the only working man on the planet who has to do the goddamn dishes. Bill could feel in his pocket the crinkle of the condom wrapper, which was beige and tattered. He grabbed his keys from the nightstand and headed downstairs.

22.

This was the kind of crap Bill hated. He mechanically shook hands with her relatives, who bore an uncanny resemblance to her. He made frequent trips to the bar and talked to the bartender as though they both were out of place with this crowd. When his conversations with people lulled, he looked out over the hedges into the dark blue sea. It was strange for him to see balding, ruddy-faced men in argyle sweaters who looked like the woman he was fucking.

2.

Sitting on a graffitied bench bolted to a yellow cement wall, Bill clasped his head between his knees. Large men with secret and some not-so-secret tattoos owned certain corners of the cell. Bill's pants were smudged around the crotch with molten lipstick. Another guy about his age who looked similarly out of place tried to piss in the rotten toilet without letting anyone see.

33.

The French doors opened out into the sun. Bill lay under the cool sheets, a naked leg hanging from the side of the bed. The bathroom door was half open. The running shower was fogging up the mirror. Bill smoked a menthol and for the first time felt what a friend once described to him as "comfortable exhaustion."

24.

Bill looked across the table at her. She was wearing one of his dress shirts. She fingered a piece of toast, laughing at something from the Comics section. He tried to look at the clock without moving his head. She looked up and saw what he was doing.

15.

Jane Fonda walked out of the men's room, tossing a mink stole around her neck. Bill followed her out thirty seconds later. He pressed a hand against the wall, holding himself up in the ill-lit hallway. The bar was packed with people. A man touched Bill on the back to signal that he wanted to squeeze past. Bill moved.

29.

In April, Bill and his ex met at the coffee shop near campus. She brought two cappuccinos and two cinnamon scones over to the table. She began talking to Bill, who kept looking around the room. Her shoulders tensed. She started in on him about how he "objectifies" women. He didn't argue but

30.

slept with a stranger later.

THE NEW RAND MCNALLY WORLD ATLAS, C6 210

Like the capital of Tadzhikistan
I long to be a name I neither know
nor can pronounce, a smeared calligraphy
of membrane and breath, an outpost of bone.
Effective immediately,
like a Hoover bagless I hereby suck
all trace of me from earth—my ramshackle
prattle marooned in some distant
acquaintance's head, my memos re:
tapioca, the coughs I've left at rest
stops, my sock puppet arsenal…
When my thumb finds the world's index
the tracks lead back to where I began.
Dushanbe is the capital of Tadzhikistan.

INDEX

Like braided rain. It was enough 15

Like crystal lining the floor, the walls, the spider webs 16

Like graphs 17

Like honey 18

Like ions 19

Like karma with a twist of lime. 20

Like larynx waterlogged 21

Like months of necks 22

Like nectar, even though I said I'd never like 23

Like things or things we say we like 24

Like Venus and its umlauts (if you are in Deutchland,
        which you're not) floating 25

Like weeks and weeks of fire. 26

Move a hair to the left. 44

Now is when you groom the monkey next to you and
        say 71

Okay, you there, 8

Oslo and all its snow is no place for 66

Please. Just take the 40

Question: have you seen my kitty? 31

Question: have you seen my longing? 65

Rank the following, where 1 = ugh, 10 = so-so: 6

Raoul, would you pass me a leg? 3

Recently it has come to our 73

Sentences that 55

The apple is huge 63
The badger is dying 50
The canary is dying 34
The dog is dying 49
The elk is dying 48
The zebra is a favorite animal of so few. 42

Ultimately, 13

Very conveniently, with toes pointing inward and nails
      firmly inserted, 59

Would you recommend 74

X-sections (that's cross-sections to you and me) but
      46

You did 68
You left me so long ago, how could I try 1

IV.

TO WHOM IT MAY CONCERN:

Ordinarily I wouldn't mention it
but What's-His-Name (You-Know-Who) claims
you're miffed by all the You-Know-What creeping
in from Who-Knows-Where. Who knows why.

What I'd like to know: have you tried
the moisturizer I sent? They say
in absence the face grows more or less etched—
presence is softer, wind-swept like
reminiscence. For example,
the guest I may have mentioned.

Who knows what any of us is looking for
anyway. Like most mothers wouldn't say
posing is sometimes okay.

       With love,

UNDERSTUDY

You enter from left, from the kitchenette.
Cross to chair. Eat before the television.
Daylight thinning. Your face and walls and throat
and fishbowl flickering. The cat licks
your soup when you arise to fix the image.
It is still snowing in Tijuana.
The steaming tacos and streets are frosted,
protagonist fleecy, slipping through people,
and when the phone rings you barely stir,
tilt head to 45° and why
is this where it seems scripted, your pause,
your questioning answering, the brevity
of the call, your return to sitting, tray
back on your lap although you've finished eating?

BILL TRANSLATES ENGLISH

Repeat this if you go missing: *My name is [your name]*.

Are the conditions good for relocating. These materials appear a bit rickety. Is this something we can fix.

Has anybody seen my kitty. He has big eyes and moves people.

Enough with the bananas. True, they are yellow and brown, mostly brown, and in bunches. We know that you are hungry, son.

There are toddlers with bottles in the distances, which drink them. They look small. Are they getting bigger. Should we do something about this.

What should we do about these people. Look at their faces. They have eaten little and need chairs. Please get them something and then sit on them.

Should I go in with these on. Are they revealing. Can you see anything. Overall, there is a sheen. Otherwise, everything is average.

I agree. Thank you so much. That makes me

think of something. Shit, what is it. Do I smell eucalyptus.

Hey, you clipped us back there. We would like you to pay. Do you have anything.

I have trouble when it is hot or cold or quiet.

Didn't you leave recently. How far you have come already. Sit down. The highway still slips into your eyes. That happens to me sometimes.

Maybe we should do something. When was the last time you were rollerskating. Yet, I do not want to scrape my face. What do you say.

It is so nice to be you. Am I forgetting something.

QUESTION

You soothe late afternoon between your hands
then snap its neck because to date its debt
for agitation is still outstanding.
Spidered light through backyard oaks might not threaten
your tiki torches, your pool's chlorine flame,
your astrochemical observations
or qualms about the health of diet shakes
but what you pin upon a bald horizon,
evening riding in, does. Anyone else lost
within this cicada-rich quilt of lawns,
the budding sky a mouth of broken teeth?
What I wouldn't give for something good to want
or eat. Eat evening. Elude the look in its eye,
release the proper mix of enzymes.

THE WEIGHT OF PAPER

Preoccupation with bureaucracy
or better yet equation of my name
with what I deem another's fate: no, these
don't eat at me although a paperweight
collection by my indiscriminate
mail slot smothers anything that claims I owe
more than seventy-six ticks a minute
or my mother a visit and Jell-O mold.

Billing flamingos tinted in. A flowered
obelisk. Dark quartz with yellow veins.
Oval. Conical. The Eiffel Tower.
Bar charts. Additions. My stark minimums.
The Sphinx is always so quick
off its stack. I know when I am licked.

HONOLULU

Your cat may have scratched open
the sky this morning
but try sneaking any of the nine
planets in your handbag through
customs. Never explain why
your carry-on is weightless.
Try. See who bites on your X-ray
of Saturn. The rings look like
ribs. The rings look like
handles. The rings look like
rings, which you'd fling over
the fence and never retrieve
from a robed and perfumed
evening introducing itself
—are we neighbors—as though
you should but never have
met under different cloud and firefly
formations. The rings look like
rings that you'd never think about
on a day when you're drinking
something like iced tea or feeling
like you're in a commercial for
iced tea. Weeds looping through,
gripping the rings—you wouldn't think
about that. They look like

adoring arms around Elvis's legs,
arms of tall people, tall because their hands
meet around what they squeeze,
which is fairly stout since
this is Elvis in 1973,
also the year the first cat batted
not .400 but the moon,
and Jupiter, security said,
had to be checked
all the way through to Honolulu.

AFTER THE DIVORCE,

after nights of whittling the frozen clouds, Bill takes in a stray, a docile, hairless creature missing a leg or two, which little affects its ability to walk like a dying garden hose. Bill only intends to dab Bactine on its pepperoni scabs, send it on its way...

But such pleasure the grateful thing takes in helping around the ravaged house! It chews back the emerald weeds sprung from the pipes and ceilings. It buffs the tile with its shiny hindquarters. It predicts storms. It drags buckets to the basement to douse the arson fires. And sometimes, though rarely, scratches to get out.

AT BEST

Sunlight clamps the grayish buildings,
swells their height. Note to self: tweak wiring
behind the cloudless backdrop, watch
as needled skyline pricks the sun with dark.

But then there is the moon to consider,
icy zipper, snared on skin. Tonight
it will awaken the latent river,
unleash it on the undressed throat of Roosevelt

Street, whose namesake may have fixed many lives
but ate mashed potatoes with a butter knife.
Candle flames swam at the roots of his half-drained
eyes and off his tongue came the dull blade.

Still the cutting edge, mulled Eleanor, doubtful,
whenever lighting was, at best, partial.

TODAY #3

Weary from revealing wrong things, today,
for good, you put a moratorium
on speech. Unscrew the bolts like stud earrings.
Extract the larynx, the maxillary
unit, the arced maw heavy in your hands
like a discovery or radiant
car part. A complaint. A question.
A relic. A curio. A boomerang.
Throw it moonward. Expect this former
messenger to be shot by all the usual
passing targets: anything feathered,
celestial, magnetic, chemical.
Expect that everything you've ever aired
comes back and you'll retract. Including that.

INTERSTATE CONSOLIDATED
TELEGRAPH OFFICE

AM IN SOME TOWN EAST OF RENO STOP
MORE SYLLABLES THAN PEOPLE STOP
WIND NEVER STOPS STOP PEEL A
CENTURY OFF WHATEVER YOU PICTURE
STOP CAN READ PEOPLE HERE
WHATEVER THAT MEANS STOP NEVER
PAID BY WORD BEFORE BUT HAD CASH
TO BURN SINCE FARED WELL AT CRAPS
STOP WHAT ARE WORDS WORTH STOP I
THE SAME PRICE AS EVERYBODY STOP
GUY HERE SAYS MAKE SHORT SWEET
STOP TO THAT I SAY SACCHARIN IS
HAPPENIN OOPS STOP WILL SLIP HIM
EXTRA FIVE FOR ALL MY JIVE STOP
STOP RHYME STOP AM PRETENDING I
LIVE HERE STOP CAN SEE MYSELF
MAKING TUMBLEWEED WREATHS BY

FIRELIGHT AND WANDERING THESE
PEAKS STOP IS IT IMPORTANT TO BE
FROM SOMEWHERE STOP GETTING
FUNNY LOOKS STOP HOPE I HAVE
ENOUGH DOUGH STOP SEE WORDS
COSTLY

BILL

V.

HOW WOULD YOU DESCRIBE HIM?

I really didn't get a good look.
Is that the standard statement you guys take?
You just want the facts from me, right Friday?
Or how about it, Dan-O: should we book
the bastard? Get this down. He wore a shirt.
If he were a pole, he'd either be
aluminum or North or ski; if a bean,
think pinto. His face may be worth

a speck more to you than my breath but less
than something you can can. Is this helping?
When you find him, twist the blade before
you pull. Make him tell what water looks
like. Make him understand that confessing
something solves nothing. Maybe let him go.

ACKNOWLEDGMENTS

Many thanks to the editors of the following publications, in which these poems first appeared (sometimes in slightly different form):

42opus: *"Hello, My Name Is"* and *"The New Rand McNally World Atlas, C6 210."*

Barrow Street: "Question"

can we have our ball back?: "Today #1," "[Tara,],"
"Beeep"

Good Foot: "Bill Translates English"

Indiana Review: "Bill Translates Hungarian," "Ordinarily #2"

The Konundrum Engine Literary Review: "Bill's Dream,"
"Hammocked, Bill," "The Weight of Paper"

The Laurel Review: "Understudy"

Meridian: "Today #2," "Today #3"

Mid-American Review: "Bill's Formal Complaint"

The National Poetry Review: "Midnight Kitchen"

Octopus: "Honolulu," "Plate 1: An Anatomy"

POOL: "Bill Translates Swedish," "Index"

Quarterly West: "The Love Life of Bill"

Quick Fiction: "[Interstate Consolidated Telegraph Office],"
"Bill," "After the divorce,"

Third Coast: "Song"

West Branch: "At Best"

Today #1," "Today #2," and "Today #3" also appeared in *SKIN*, a letterpress, bilingual chapbook produced in collaboration with book artist Steve Miller, Cuban artist Julio César Peña Peralta, and translator Maria Vargas (Red Hydra Press, 2005).

"Bill" also appeared in *Flash Fiction Forward* (W.W. Norton & Company, 2006). Robert Shapard and James Thomas, eds.

"Bill's Formal Complaint" received an AWP Intro Journals Award for poetry (2002).

"Bill's Formal Complaint" also appeared as a limited-edition broadside published by Daniel Urban and April Rohn (2002).

Thanks also to Susie, CJ Sage, Hailey Leithauser, Robin Behn, Joel Brouwer, Michael Martone, Wendy Rawlings, and Bruce Smith.

Printed in the United States
106735LV00002B/1-3/P